50 Rice Dishes for Every Cuisine

By: Kelly Johnson

Table of Contents

- Biryani (Indian)
- Paella (Spanish)
- Risotto (Italian)
- Fried Rice (Chinese)
- Jollof Rice (West African)
- Arroz con Pollo (Latin American)
- Sushi (Japanese)
- Dolma (Turkish)
- Pilaf (Middle Eastern)
- Congee (Chinese)
- Nasi Goreng (Indonesian)
- Coconut Rice (Caribbean)
- Khao Pad (Thai Fried Rice)
- Rice and Beans (Caribbean)
- Lemon Rice (Indian)
- Risotto alla Milanese (Italian)
- Khichdi (Indian)
- Loco Moco (Hawaiian)
- Spanish Rice (Mexican)
- Zucchini Rice (Mediterranean)
- Shrimp Fried Rice (Chinese)
- Saffron Rice (Persian)
- Methi Rice (Indian)
- Risi e Bisi (Italian)
- Cheesy Mexican Rice (Mexican)
- Vegetable Biryani (Indian)
- Cajun Dirty Rice (Southern U.S.)
- Fried Rice Balls (Japanese)
- Pesto Rice (Italian)
- Arroz Verde (Mexican)
- Cilantro Lime Rice (Mexican)
- Caprese Risotto (Italian)
- Persian Jeweled Rice (Iranian)
- Mango Sticky Rice (Thai)
- Risotto al Nero di Seppia (Italian)
- Lemon Herb Rice (Mediterranean)

- Arroz de Marisco (Portuguese)
- Basmati Rice with Cardamom (Indian)
- Peas and Rice (Jamaican)
- Coconut Mango Rice (Caribbean)
- Curried Rice (Indian)
- Brown Rice Sushi (Japanese)
- Spanish Fideuà (Spanish)
- Tabbouleh (Middle Eastern)
- Cheddar Rice (Southern U.S.)
- Prawn Risotto (Italian)
- Garlic Rice (Filipino)
- Egg Fried Rice (Chinese)
- Sticky Rice with Pork (Laotian)
- Vegetable Fried Rice (Asian Fusion)

Biryani (Indian)

Ingredients:

- **For the Marinade:**
    - 1 lb (450g) chicken (or lamb/beef)
    - 1 cup yogurt
    - 2 large onions, thinly sliced
    - 2 tomatoes, chopped
    - 2-3 green chilies, slit
    - 1 tablespoon ginger-garlic paste
    - 1 teaspoon red chili powder
    - 1 teaspoon turmeric powder
    - 1 tablespoon garam masala
    - Salt, to taste
    - 1/4 cup fresh mint leaves, chopped
    - 1/4 cup fresh coriander leaves, chopped
    - 2 tablespoons lemon juice
- **For the Rice:**
    - 2 cups basmati rice
    - 4 cups water
    - 4-5 green cardamom pods
    - 4-5 cloves
    - 1-2 bay leaves
    - 1 cinnamon stick
    - Salt, to taste
- **For Assembling:**
    - 2-3 tablespoons ghee or cooking oil
    - Fried onions (store-bought or homemade)
    - Additional mint and coriander for garnish

Instructions:

1. **Marinate the Meat:**
    - In a large bowl, combine yogurt, ginger-garlic paste, red chili powder, turmeric powder, garam masala, salt, chopped mint, coriander, green chilies, and lemon juice.
    - Add the chicken (or lamb/beef) and mix well. Cover and refrigerate for at least 1 hour (preferably overnight).
2. **Prepare the Rice:**
    - Rinse the basmati rice in cold water until the water runs clear. Soak the rice in water for about 30 minutes, then drain.
    - In a large pot, bring 4 cups of water to a boil. Add cardamom, cloves, bay leaves, cinnamon, and salt.

- Once boiling, add the soaked rice and cook until it's about 70% done. Drain and set aside.
3. **Cook the Marinated Meat:**
    - In a heavy-bottomed pot, heat ghee or oil over medium heat. Add sliced onions and sauté until golden brown.
    - Add the marinated meat to the pot and cook until it's browned and cooked through, about 10-15 minutes. Stir occasionally.
4. **Layer the Biryani:**
    - Once the meat is cooked, spread half of the cooked rice over the meat in the pot. Sprinkle half of the fried onions, mint, and coriander.
    - Layer the remaining rice on top and finish with the remaining fried onions, mint, and coriander.
5. **Dum Cooking:**
    - Cover the pot with a tight-fitting lid. You can seal the edges with dough (optional) to prevent steam from escaping.
    - Cook on low heat for about 20-30 minutes to allow the flavors to meld (this is called "dum").
6. **Serve:**
    - Gently fluff the biryani before serving. Serve hot with raita (yogurt sauce) or salad on the side.

Paella (Spanish)

Ingredients:

- **For the Paella:**
    - 2 cups short-grain rice (like Bomba or Arborio)
    - 4 cups chicken or seafood broth
    - 1 lb (450g) chicken, cut into pieces
    - 1 lb (450g) seafood (shrimp, mussels, calamari)
    - 1 onion, finely chopped
    - 2 cloves garlic, minced
    - 1 bell pepper, chopped
    - 1 can (14 oz) diced tomatoes
    - 1 teaspoon smoked paprika
    - 1/2 teaspoon saffron threads
    - Olive oil, for cooking
    - Salt and pepper, to taste
    - Fresh parsley, chopped, for garnish
    - Lemon wedges, for serving

Instructions:

1. In a large paella pan or a wide skillet, heat olive oil over medium heat. Add chicken pieces and brown on all sides. Remove and set aside.
2. In the same pan, add chopped onion, garlic, and bell pepper. Sauté until softened. Stir in diced tomatoes, paprika, and saffron. Cook for a few minutes.
3. Add the rice and stir well to coat. Pour in the broth and bring to a simmer. Add the chicken back to the pan.
4. After about 10 minutes of cooking, arrange the seafood on top of the rice. Do not stir after adding seafood. Cook until the rice is tender and the liquid is absorbed, about 15-20 minutes.
5. Remove from heat and let rest for a few minutes. Garnish with fresh parsley and serve with lemon wedges.

Risotto (Italian)

Ingredients:

- **For the Risotto:**
    - 1 1/2 cups Arborio rice
    - 4 cups chicken or vegetable broth
    - 1 cup dry white wine
    - 1 onion, finely chopped
    - 2 cloves garlic, minced
    - 1 cup grated Parmesan cheese
    - 2 tablespoons butter
    - Olive oil, for cooking
    - Salt and pepper, to taste
    - Fresh parsley, chopped, for garnish

Instructions:

1. In a saucepan, keep the broth warm over low heat.
2. In a large skillet, heat olive oil and 1 tablespoon of butter over medium heat. Add chopped onion and garlic, sauté until translucent.
3. Stir in the Arborio rice and cook for about 2-3 minutes until lightly toasted.
4. Pour in the white wine and cook, stirring frequently, until it's mostly absorbed.
5. Begin adding warm broth, one ladle at a time, stirring constantly. Wait until the liquid is absorbed before adding more. Continue this process for about 18-20 minutes, until the rice is creamy and al dente.
6. Stir in the remaining butter and grated Parmesan cheese. Season with salt and pepper. Garnish with fresh parsley and serve hot.

Fried Rice (Chinese)

Ingredients:

- **For the Fried Rice:**
    - 3 cups cooked rice (preferably day-old)
    - 2 tablespoons vegetable oil
    - 2 eggs, beaten
    - 1 cup mixed vegetables (carrots, peas, bell peppers)
    - 2-3 green onions, chopped
    - 3 tablespoons soy sauce
    - 1 teaspoon sesame oil
    - Salt and pepper, to taste

Instructions:

1. Make sure the rice is cold and separated. This helps to prevent clumping.
2. In a large skillet or wok, heat 1 tablespoon of vegetable oil over medium-high heat. Add the beaten eggs and scramble until cooked. Remove and set aside.
3. In the same pan, add the remaining oil. Add mixed vegetables and stir-fry for 2-3 minutes until tender.
4. Add the cooked rice to the pan, breaking up any clumps. Stir-fry for about 5 minutes, allowing it to heat through.
5. Add scrambled eggs, green onions, soy sauce, and sesame oil. Stir well to combine. Season with salt and pepper to taste.
6. Serve hot as a side dish or main course.

Jollof Rice (West African)

Ingredients:

- 2 cups long-grain parboiled rice
- 1/4 cup vegetable oil
- 1 onion, chopped
- 2-3 tomatoes, blended
- 1 red bell pepper, blended
- 1 teaspoon tomato paste
- 2-3 cups chicken or vegetable broth
- 1 teaspoon thyme
- 1 teaspoon curry powder
- 2-3 bay leaves
- Salt and pepper, to taste
- 1 cup mixed vegetables (peas, carrots, etc.)
- Optional: cooked chicken or shrimp for serving

Instructions:

1. Heat vegetable oil in a large pot. Add chopped onion and sauté until translucent.
2. Stir in blended tomatoes, red bell pepper, and tomato paste. Cook until the sauce reduces and thickens.
3. Add the rice, broth, thyme, curry powder, bay leaves, salt, and pepper. Stir well.
4. Bring to a boil, then reduce heat to low. Cover and simmer for about 20-30 minutes, until the rice is cooked and liquid is absorbed.
5. Add mixed vegetables and cooked chicken or shrimp if desired. Stir gently and cook for an additional 5 minutes.
6. Fluff the rice and serve hot.

Arroz con Pollo (Latin American)

Ingredients:

- 2 cups long-grain rice
- 1 lb (450g) chicken, cut into pieces
- 1/4 cup vegetable oil
- 1 onion, chopped
- 2 cloves garlic, minced
- 1 bell pepper, chopped
- 1 can (14 oz) diced tomatoes
- 2-3 cups chicken broth
- 1 teaspoon cumin
- 1 teaspoon paprika
- Salt and pepper, to taste
- 1 cup frozen peas
- Fresh cilantro, for garnish

Instructions:

1. In a large pot, heat oil over medium heat. Add chicken and brown on all sides. Remove and set aside.
2. In the same pot, add onion, garlic, and bell pepper. Sauté until softened.
3. Stir in diced tomatoes, rice, cumin, paprika, salt, and pepper. Mix well.
4. Return the chicken to the pot and add chicken broth. Bring to a boil.
5. Reduce heat to low, cover, and simmer for about 25-30 minutes, until the rice is cooked and chicken is tender.
6. Stir in frozen peas and let sit covered for a few minutes. Garnish with fresh cilantro and serve.

Sushi (Japanese)

Ingredients:

- 2 cups sushi rice
- 2 1/2 cups water
- 1/3 cup rice vinegar
- 3 tablespoons sugar
- 1 teaspoon salt
- Nori sheets
- Fillings (cucumber, avocado, crab, etc.)
- Soy sauce, for serving

Instructions:

1. Rinse sushi rice under cold water until the water runs clear. Combine rice and water in a pot and bring to a boil. Reduce heat, cover, and simmer for 20 minutes. Remove from heat and let it sit covered for 10 minutes.
2. In a small saucepan, heat rice vinegar, sugar, and salt until dissolved. Stir into the cooked rice.
3. Place a nori sheet on a bamboo mat. Spread a thin layer of rice, leaving a border. Arrange desired fillings in the center.
4. Roll the sushi tightly using the mat. Slice into pieces with a sharp knife.
5. Serve with soy sauce for dipping.

Dolma (Turkish)

Ingredients:

- 1 cup rice
- 1/2 lb (225g) ground meat (beef or lamb)
- 1 onion, chopped
- 2-3 tablespoons pine nuts
- 1/4 cup raisins (optional)
- 1/4 cup fresh parsley, chopped
- 1 teaspoon cinnamon
- Salt and pepper, to taste
- Grape leaves (canned or fresh)
- 2 cups chicken or vegetable broth

Instructions:

1. In a skillet, sauté onion and pine nuts until golden. Add ground meat and cook until browned. Stir in rice, raisins, parsley, cinnamon, salt, and pepper. Add a little broth and cook until rice is partially cooked.
2. Rinse grape leaves and lay them flat. Place a spoonful of filling at the base of each leaf and roll tightly, tucking in the sides.
3. Place dolmas in a pot, seam-side down. Pour broth over them and bring to a boil.
4. Reduce heat to low, cover, and simmer for about 30-40 minutes until rice is fully cooked.
5. Serve warm or at room temperature.

Pilaf (Middle Eastern)

Ingredients:

- 1 1/2 cups long-grain rice
- 3 cups chicken or vegetable broth
- 1/4 cup butter or olive oil
- 1 onion, chopped
- 2 cloves garlic, minced
- 1 teaspoon cumin
- 1/2 teaspoon cinnamon
- Salt and pepper, to taste
- Optional: toasted nuts and dried fruits for garnish

Instructions:

1. In a large pot, heat butter or olive oil over medium heat. Add chopped onion and garlic, sauté until softened.
2. Stir in rice and cook for a few minutes until lightly toasted.
3. Add broth, cumin, cinnamon, salt, and pepper. Bring to a boil.
4. Reduce heat to low, cover, and simmer for about 18-20 minutes until rice is tender and liquid is absorbed.
5. Fluff the rice with a fork and garnish with toasted nuts and dried fruits if desired.

Congee (Chinese)

Ingredients:

- 1 cup rice
- 8 cups water or broth
- Salt, to taste
- Optional toppings: sliced green onions, pickled vegetables, soy sauce, shredded chicken, or century eggs

Instructions:

1. Rinse rice under cold water until the water runs clear.
2. In a large pot, combine rice and water or broth. Bring to a boil.
3. Reduce heat to low and simmer, stirring occasionally, for about 1-1.5 hours until the rice breaks down and the mixture thickens.
4. Season with salt and serve hot with desired toppings.

Nasi Goreng (Indonesian)

Ingredients:

- 3 cups cooked rice (preferably day-old)
- 2 tablespoons vegetable oil
- 2 cloves garlic, minced
- 2-3 shallots, minced
- 1 cup mixed vegetables (carrots, peas, etc.)
- 2-3 tablespoons soy sauce
- 1 tablespoon sweet soy sauce (kecap manis)
- 2 eggs, beaten
- Optional: cooked shrimp or chicken, sliced cucumber, and fried shallots for garnish

Instructions:

1. In a large skillet or wok, heat vegetable oil over medium-high heat. Add garlic and shallots, sauté until fragrant.
2. Add mixed vegetables and stir-fry for a few minutes.
3. Push the vegetables to one side of the pan. Pour in the beaten eggs and scramble until cooked.
4. Add the cooked rice, soy sauce, and sweet soy sauce. Stir-fry everything together until heated through.
5. Serve hot, garnished with cucumber slices and fried shallots if desired.

Coconut Rice (Caribbean)

Ingredients:

- 2 cups long-grain rice
- 1 can (13.5 oz) coconut milk
- 1 cup water
- 1 teaspoon salt
- Optional: lime zest or fresh herbs for garnish

Instructions:

1. Rinse the rice under cold water until the water runs clear.
2. In a pot, combine coconut milk, water, salt, and the rinsed rice.
3. Bring to a boil, then reduce heat to low, cover, and simmer for about 20-25 minutes until the rice is cooked and liquid is absorbed.
4. Fluff the rice with a fork and garnish with lime zest or fresh herbs if desired.

Khao Pad (Thai Fried Rice)

Ingredients:

- 2 cups jasmine rice, cooked and cooled
- 2 tablespoons vegetable oil
- 2 cloves garlic, minced
- 1 onion, chopped
- 2 eggs, beaten
- 1 cup mixed vegetables (carrots, peas, corn)
- 3 tablespoons soy sauce
- 1 tablespoon fish sauce
- 1 teaspoon sugar
- 2 green onions, chopped
- Fresh cilantro, for garnish
- Lime wedges, for serving

Instructions:

1. Heat vegetable oil in a large wok or skillet over medium heat. Add garlic and onion, sauté until fragrant.
2. Push the vegetables to the side and pour in the beaten eggs. Scramble until fully cooked.
3. Add mixed vegetables and stir-fry for a few minutes.
4. Add cooked rice, soy sauce, fish sauce, and sugar. Stir well and cook until heated through.
5. Stir in chopped green onions and garnish with cilantro. Serve with lime wedges.

Rice and Beans (Caribbean)

Ingredients:

- 1 cup long-grain rice
- 1 can (15 oz) black beans, drained and rinsed
- 1 cup coconut milk
- 1 cup vegetable broth or water
- 1 onion, chopped
- 2 cloves garlic, minced
- 1 teaspoon thyme
- 1 teaspoon cumin
- Salt and pepper, to taste
- Optional: chopped green onions and cilantro for garnish

Instructions:

1. In a large pot, heat some oil over medium heat. Add onion and garlic, sauté until softened.
2. Stir in rice, black beans, coconut milk, broth, thyme, cumin, salt, and pepper.
3. Bring to a boil, then reduce heat to low. Cover and simmer for about 20-25 minutes, until rice is cooked and liquid is absorbed.
4. Fluff the rice with a fork and garnish with green onions and cilantro if desired.

Lemon Rice (Indian)

Ingredients:

- 2 cups cooked rice
- 2 tablespoons vegetable oil
- 1 teaspoon mustard seeds
- 1 teaspoon turmeric powder
- 2-3 green chilies, slit
- 1/4 cup peanuts or cashews
- Juice of 1 lemon
- Salt, to taste
- Fresh cilantro, for garnish

Instructions:

1. Heat oil in a pan over medium heat. Add mustard seeds and let them splutter.
2. Stir in turmeric, green chilies, and peanuts. Sauté for a few minutes until the peanuts are golden.
3. Add the cooked rice and salt, mixing well to combine.
4. Squeeze in lemon juice and mix gently. Garnish with cilantro and serve.

Risotto alla Milanese (Italian)

Ingredients:

- 1 cup Arborio rice
- 4 cups chicken or vegetable broth
- 1/2 cup dry white wine
- 1 onion, finely chopped
- 2 tablespoons butter
- 1 tablespoon olive oil
- 1/4 teaspoon saffron threads
- 1/2 cup grated Parmesan cheese
- Salt and pepper, to taste
- Fresh parsley, for garnish

Instructions:

1. In a saucepan, heat the broth and add saffron. Keep warm over low heat.
2. In a separate pot, heat olive oil and butter. Add onion and sauté until translucent.
3. Stir in Arborio rice, cooking for 1-2 minutes until lightly toasted.
4. Add white wine and stir until absorbed. Gradually add the broth, one ladle at a time, stirring continuously until absorbed before adding more.
5. Cook until rice is creamy and al dente. Stir in Parmesan cheese, salt, and pepper. Garnish with parsley and serve.

Khichdi (Indian)

Ingredients:

- 1 cup rice
- 1/2 cup split yellow lentils (moong dal)
- 4 cups water
- 1 teaspoon turmeric powder
- 1 teaspoon cumin seeds
- 1 onion, chopped
- 2-3 green chilies, slit
- 2 tablespoons ghee or oil
- Salt, to taste
- Fresh cilantro, for garnish

Instructions:

1. Rinse rice and lentils together until water runs clear.
2. In a pressure cooker or pot, heat ghee or oil. Add cumin seeds, onion, and green chilies. Sauté until onions are golden.
3. Add rice, lentils, turmeric, salt, and water. Stir well.
4. If using a pressure cooker, cook for 3-4 whistles. In a pot, simmer covered until rice and lentils are soft.
5. Garnish with cilantro and serve hot.

Loco Moco (Hawaiian)

Ingredients:

- 2 cups cooked rice
- 1 lb (450g) ground beef
- 2 eggs
- 1/4 cup onion, finely chopped
- 2 tablespoons soy sauce
- 1 cup beef broth
- 1 tablespoon cornstarch (optional, for thickening)
- Salt and pepper, to taste
- Green onions, for garnish

Instructions:

1. Form ground beef into patties and season with salt and pepper. Cook in a skillet over medium heat until browned on both sides. Remove and set aside.
2. In the same skillet, sauté onion until softened. Add beef broth and soy sauce. Simmer for a few minutes.
3. If desired, mix cornstarch with a little water and add to the broth to thicken.
4. In a separate pan, fry eggs to desired doneness.
5. To serve, place a scoop of rice on a plate, top with a burger patty, a fried egg, and drizzle with gravy. Garnish with green onions.

Spanish Rice (Mexican)

Ingredients:

- 2 cups long-grain rice
- 1/4 cup vegetable oil
- 1 onion, chopped
- 2 cloves garlic, minced
- 1 can (14 oz) diced tomatoes
- 3 cups chicken or vegetable broth
- 1 teaspoon cumin
- 1 teaspoon chili powder
- Salt, to taste
- Fresh cilantro, for garnish

Instructions:

1. Heat oil in a large pot over medium heat. Add onion and garlic, sauté until softened.
2. Stir in rice, cooking for 2-3 minutes until lightly toasted.
3. Add diced tomatoes, broth, cumin, chili powder, and salt. Bring to a boil.
4. Reduce heat to low, cover, and simmer for about 20-25 minutes until rice is cooked and liquid is absorbed.
5. Fluff the rice and garnish with fresh cilantro before serving.

Zucchini Rice (Mediterranean)

Ingredients:

- 2 cups cooked rice
- 1 medium zucchini, grated
- 2 tablespoons olive oil
- 1 onion, chopped
- 2 cloves garlic, minced
- 1 teaspoon oregano
- Salt and pepper, to taste
- Optional: crumbled feta cheese and fresh parsley for garnish

Instructions:

1. In a large skillet, heat olive oil over medium heat. Add onion and garlic, sauté until softened.
2. Stir in grated zucchini and cook for a few minutes until tender.
3. Add cooked rice, oregano, salt, and pepper. Mix well and cook until heated through.
4. Serve garnished with crumbled feta and fresh parsley if desired.

Shrimp Fried Rice (Chinese)

Ingredients:

- 2 cups cooked rice, cooled
- 1/2 lb (225g) shrimp, peeled and deveined
- 2 tablespoons vegetable oil
- 2 cloves garlic, minced
- 1 onion, chopped
- 2 eggs, beaten
- 1 cup mixed vegetables (peas, carrots, bell peppers)
- 3 tablespoons soy sauce
- 1 tablespoon oyster sauce (optional)
- Salt and pepper, to taste
- Green onions, for garnish

Instructions:

1. Heat vegetable oil in a large skillet or wok over medium heat. Add garlic and onion, sauté until fragrant.
2. Add shrimp and cook until pink. Push shrimp to the side and pour in the beaten eggs, scrambling until fully cooked.
3. Stir in mixed vegetables and cooked rice, mixing well.
4. Add soy sauce, oyster sauce, salt, and pepper. Stir until heated through.
5. Garnish with chopped green onions and serve hot.

Saffron Rice (Persian)

Ingredients:

- 2 cups basmati rice
- 4 cups water
- 1/4 teaspoon saffron threads
- 2 tablespoons butter or oil
- 1 onion, chopped
- 1/2 teaspoon turmeric powder
- Salt, to taste
- Optional: slivered almonds and dried raisins for garnish

Instructions:

1. Rinse basmati rice under cold water until the water runs clear. Soak for 30 minutes, then drain.
2. In a saucepan, heat butter or oil over medium heat. Add chopped onion and sauté until golden.
3. Add turmeric and saffron, stirring for a minute. Then, add the soaked rice and water with salt.
4. Bring to a boil, reduce heat to low, cover, and cook for about 20 minutes until rice is tender and water is absorbed.
5. Fluff with a fork and serve, garnished with almonds and raisins if desired.

Methi Rice (Indian)

Ingredients:

- 2 cups cooked rice
- 1 cup fresh fenugreek leaves (methi), chopped
- 2 tablespoons oil or ghee
- 1 teaspoon cumin seeds
- 1 onion, sliced
- 2 green chilies, slit
- 1/2 teaspoon turmeric powder
- Salt, to taste

Instructions:

1. Heat oil or ghee in a pan over medium heat. Add cumin seeds and let them splutter.
2. Add sliced onion and green chilies, sautéing until onions are soft.
3. Stir in fenugreek leaves, turmeric powder, and salt. Cook until the leaves wilt.
4. Add cooked rice, mixing gently to combine. Cook for a few more minutes until heated through.
5. Serve hot as a side dish or main course.

Risi e Bisi (Italian)

Ingredients:

- 1 cup Arborio rice
- 4 cups vegetable or chicken broth
- 1/2 cup peas (fresh or frozen)
- 1 onion, chopped
- 1/4 cup pancetta or bacon, diced (optional)
- 1/2 cup Parmesan cheese, grated
- 2 tablespoons butter
- Salt and pepper, to taste
- Fresh parsley, for garnish

Instructions:

1. In a saucepan, heat broth and keep warm over low heat.
2. In a separate pot, sauté pancetta (if using) until crispy. Add onion and cook until soft.
3. Stir in Arborio rice, cooking for 1-2 minutes until slightly toasted.
4. Add broth one ladle at a time, stirring until absorbed before adding more.
5. When rice is nearly cooked, stir in peas, butter, and Parmesan cheese. Season with salt and pepper.
6. Garnish with parsley and serve immediately.

Cheesy Mexican Rice (Mexican)

Ingredients:

- 2 cups long-grain rice
- 1/4 cup vegetable oil
- 1 onion, chopped
- 2 cloves garlic, minced
- 1 can (14 oz) diced tomatoes
- 3 cups chicken or vegetable broth
- 1 teaspoon cumin
- 1/2 cup shredded cheese (cheddar or Monterey Jack)
- Salt and pepper, to taste
- Fresh cilantro, for garnish

Instructions:

1. In a large pot, heat oil over medium heat. Add onion and garlic, sauté until softened.
2. Stir in rice, cooking for 2-3 minutes until lightly toasted.
3. Add diced tomatoes, broth, cumin, salt, and pepper. Bring to a boil.
4. Reduce heat to low, cover, and simmer for about 20-25 minutes until rice is cooked and liquid is absorbed.
5. Stir in shredded cheese until melted. Garnish with cilantro and serve.

Vegetable Biryani (Indian)

Ingredients:

- 2 cups basmati rice
- 4 cups water
- 1 cup mixed vegetables (carrots, peas, beans)
- 1 onion, thinly sliced
- 2 tablespoons oil or ghee
- 2 teaspoons ginger-garlic paste
- 2-3 green chilies, slit
- 1 teaspoon biryani masala (or garam masala)
- Salt, to taste
- Fresh cilantro and mint for garnish

Instructions:

1. Rinse basmati rice under cold water until the water runs clear. Soak for 30 minutes, then drain.
2. In a large pot, heat oil or ghee. Add sliced onions and sauté until golden brown.
3. Stir in ginger-garlic paste and green chilies, cooking for a minute.
4. Add mixed vegetables, biryani masala, and salt. Cook for a few minutes until vegetables are tender.
5. Add soaked rice and water, bring to a boil, then reduce heat to low. Cover and cook for about 20 minutes until rice is cooked and water is absorbed.
6. Fluff the rice and garnish with cilantro and mint before serving.

Cajun Dirty Rice (Southern U.S.)

Ingredients:

- 1 cup long-grain rice
- 1/2 lb (225g) ground beef or sausage
- 1/4 cup onion, chopped
- 1/4 cup bell pepper, chopped
- 1/4 cup celery, chopped
- 2 cloves garlic, minced
- 2 cups chicken broth
- 1 tablespoon Cajun seasoning
- Salt and pepper, to taste
- Green onions, for garnish

Instructions:

1. In a large skillet, cook ground beef or sausage over medium heat until browned. Drain excess fat.
2. Add onion, bell pepper, celery, and garlic, sautéing until vegetables are tender.
3. Stir in rice, Cajun seasoning, salt, and pepper.
4. Add chicken broth and bring to a boil. Reduce heat to low, cover, and simmer for about 20-25 minutes until rice is cooked and liquid is absorbed.
5. Fluff the rice and garnish with chopped green onions before serving.

Fried Rice Balls (Japanese)

Ingredients:

- 2 cups cooked rice
- 1/2 cup vegetables (carrots, peas, corn), finely chopped
- 1/4 cup green onions, chopped
- 1 egg, beaten
- 1/4 cup breadcrumbs
- 1 tablespoon soy sauce
- Oil, for frying
- Salt and pepper, to taste

Instructions:

1. In a bowl, combine cooked rice, vegetables, green onions, egg, soy sauce, salt, and pepper. Mix well.
2. Form the mixture into small balls, then roll each in breadcrumbs.
3. Heat oil in a frying pan over medium heat. Fry the rice balls until golden brown and crispy on all sides.
4. Drain on paper towels and serve warm with dipping sauce.

Pesto Rice (Italian)

Ingredients:

- 2 cups cooked rice
- 1/4 cup pesto sauce
- 1/4 cup Parmesan cheese, grated
- 1/2 cup cherry tomatoes, halved
- Salt and pepper, to taste
- Fresh basil, for garnish

Instructions:

1. In a large bowl, combine the cooked rice and pesto sauce. Mix well.
2. Stir in Parmesan cheese and cherry tomatoes. Season with salt and pepper to taste.
3. Serve warm, garnished with fresh basil.

Arroz Verde (Mexican)

Ingredients:

- 2 cups long-grain rice
- 4 cups vegetable or chicken broth
- 1 cup fresh cilantro, chopped
- 1/2 cup green onions, chopped
- 1/4 cup jalapeño, chopped (optional)
- 2 tablespoons oil
- Salt, to taste

Instructions:

1. In a blender, combine cilantro, green onions, jalapeño, and 1 cup of broth. Blend until smooth.
2. In a pot, heat oil over medium heat. Add rice and toast for a few minutes.
3. Pour in the blended mixture and remaining broth. Add salt to taste.
4. Bring to a boil, then reduce heat to low. Cover and cook for about 20 minutes until rice is tender.
5. Fluff with a fork and serve.

Cilantro Lime Rice (Mexican)

Ingredients:

- 2 cups cooked rice
- Juice of 1 lime
- 1/4 cup fresh cilantro, chopped
- 1 tablespoon olive oil
- Salt, to taste

Instructions:

1. In a large bowl, combine cooked rice, lime juice, cilantro, and olive oil.
2. Season with salt to taste and mix well.
3. Serve warm as a side dish.

Caprese Risotto (Italian)

Ingredients:

- 1 cup Arborio rice
- 4 cups vegetable or chicken broth
- 1 cup cherry tomatoes, halved
- 1/2 cup fresh mozzarella, diced
- 1/4 cup fresh basil, chopped
- 1/2 onion, chopped
- 2 tablespoons olive oil
- Salt and pepper, to taste

Instructions:

1. In a saucepan, heat broth and keep warm over low heat.
2. In a separate pot, heat olive oil. Add onion and sauté until soft.
3. Stir in Arborio rice and cook for 1-2 minutes until slightly toasted.
4. Gradually add broth, one ladle at a time, stirring until absorbed.
5. When rice is nearly cooked, stir in cherry tomatoes, mozzarella, and basil. Season with salt and pepper.
6. Serve hot.

Persian Jeweled Rice (Iranian)

Ingredients:

- 2 cups basmati rice
- 4 cups water
- 1/2 cup dried fruits (barberries, raisins, or apricots)
- 1/2 cup slivered almonds or pistachios
- 1/4 teaspoon saffron threads
- 2 tablespoons butter
- 1 onion, chopped
- 1 teaspoon cinnamon
- Salt, to taste

Instructions:

1. Rinse basmati rice under cold water until the water runs clear. Soak for 30 minutes, then drain.
2. In a pot, heat butter and sauté onion until golden.
3. Stir in cinnamon and dried fruits, cooking for a few minutes.
4. Add rice, water, saffron, and salt. Bring to a boil, then reduce heat to low. Cover and cook for about 20 minutes until rice is tender.
5. Fluff with a fork and mix in slivered almonds or pistachios before serving.

Mango Sticky Rice (Thai)

Ingredients:

- 1 cup glutinous rice
- 1 1/2 cups coconut milk
- 1/2 cup sugar
- 1/4 teaspoon salt
- 2 ripe mangoes, sliced
- Sesame seeds or mung beans for garnish (optional)

Instructions:

1. Soak glutinous rice in water for at least 3 hours, then drain.
2. Steam rice in a bamboo steamer for about 30 minutes until tender.
3. In a saucepan, heat coconut milk, sugar, and salt until dissolved. Reserve a little for drizzling.
4. Mix cooked rice with the coconut milk mixture, letting it sit for 30 minutes.
5. Serve sticky rice with sliced mango on the side, drizzled with reserved coconut milk. Garnish if desired.

Risotto al Nero di Seppia (Italian)

Ingredients:

- 1 cup Arborio rice
- 4 cups fish or vegetable broth
- 1/2 cup white wine
- 2-3 oz cuttlefish or squid ink
- 1 onion, chopped
- 2 tablespoons olive oil
- Salt and pepper, to taste
- Fresh parsley, for garnish

Instructions:

1. In a saucepan, heat broth and keep warm over low heat.
2. In a separate pot, heat olive oil. Add onion and sauté until soft.
3. Stir in Arborio rice and cook for 1-2 minutes until slightly toasted.
4. Add white wine and cook until absorbed. Gradually add broth, one ladle at a time, stirring until absorbed.
5. When rice is nearly cooked, stir in cuttlefish or squid ink, seasoning with salt and pepper.
6. Serve hot, garnished with fresh parsley.

Lemon Herb Rice (Mediterranean)

Ingredients:

- 2 cups long-grain rice
- 4 cups vegetable or chicken broth
- Juice and zest of 1 lemon
- 1/4 cup fresh parsley, chopped
- 1/4 cup olive oil
- Salt and pepper, to taste

Instructions:

1. In a pot, heat olive oil over medium heat. Add rice and toast for a few minutes.
2. Add broth, lemon juice, lemon zest, salt, and pepper. Bring to a boil.
3. Reduce heat to low, cover, and simmer for about 20 minutes until rice is cooked.
4. Fluff with a fork and stir in parsley before serving.

Arroz de Marisco (Portuguese)

Ingredients:

- 2 cups short-grain rice
- 4 cups seafood broth
- 1 lb mixed seafood (shrimp, clams, mussels)
- 1 onion, chopped
- 2 cloves garlic, minced
- 1/2 bell pepper, chopped
- 1 tomato, diced
- 1/4 cup olive oil
- 1 teaspoon paprika
- Salt and pepper, to taste
- Fresh parsley, for garnish

Instructions:

1. In a large pot, heat olive oil over medium heat. Add onion, garlic, and bell pepper. Sauté until soft.
2. Stir in diced tomato and paprika. Cook for a few minutes.
3. Add rice and seafood broth. Bring to a boil, then reduce heat to low and simmer for about 15 minutes.
4. Add mixed seafood, cover, and cook for an additional 10-15 minutes until the seafood is cooked and rice is tender.
5. Season with salt and pepper. Garnish with fresh parsley before serving.

Basmati Rice with Cardamom (Indian)

Ingredients:

- 2 cups basmati rice
- 4 cups water
- 4-5 green cardamom pods
- 1/2 teaspoon salt
- 2 tablespoons ghee or oil

Instructions:

1. Rinse basmati rice under cold water until the water runs clear. Soak for 30 minutes, then drain.
2. In a pot, heat ghee or oil. Add cardamom pods and sauté for a minute.
3. Add rice and toast for 1-2 minutes.
4. Pour in water and add salt. Bring to a boil, then reduce heat to low. Cover and cook for about 15-20 minutes until rice is tender and water is absorbed.
5. Fluff with a fork and serve.

Peas and Rice (Jamaican)

Ingredients:

- 2 cups long-grain rice
- 1 can (15 oz) coconut milk
- 1 cup vegetable or chicken broth
- 1 cup green peas (fresh or frozen)
- 1 onion, chopped
- 2 cloves garlic, minced
- 1 teaspoon thyme
- Salt and pepper, to taste

Instructions:

1. In a pot, heat a bit of oil over medium heat. Add onion and garlic, sautéing until soft.
2. Stir in rice, coconut milk, broth, peas, and thyme. Season with salt and pepper.
3. Bring to a boil, then reduce heat to low. Cover and cook for about 20 minutes until rice is tender.
4. Fluff with a fork and serve.

Coconut Mango Rice (Caribbean)

Ingredients:

- 2 cups jasmine rice
- 1 can (13.5 oz) coconut milk
- 1 cup water
- 1 ripe mango, diced
- 1/4 cup sugar (optional)
- Salt, to taste

Instructions:

1. Rinse jasmine rice under cold water until clear. Drain.
2. In a pot, combine coconut milk, water, sugar, and salt. Bring to a boil.
3. Stir in rice and reduce heat to low. Cover and cook for about 15-20 minutes until rice is tender.
4. Once cooked, fluff the rice and mix in diced mango. Serve warm.

Curried Rice (Indian)

Ingredients:

- 2 cups long-grain rice
- 4 cups water
- 1 onion, chopped
- 2 cloves garlic, minced
- 1 tablespoon curry powder
- 1/2 cup peas (fresh or frozen)
- 2 tablespoons oil
- Salt, to taste

Instructions:

1. In a pot, heat oil over medium heat. Add onion and garlic, sautéing until soft.
2. Stir in curry powder and cook for another minute.
3. Add rice, water, and salt. Bring to a boil, then reduce heat to low. Cover and simmer for about 20 minutes until rice is tender.
4. Stir in peas and cook for an additional 5 minutes. Fluff with a fork before serving.

Brown Rice Sushi (Japanese)

Ingredients:

- 2 cups brown rice
- 2 1/2 cups water
- 1/4 cup rice vinegar
- 1 tablespoon sugar
- 1 teaspoon salt
- Nori sheets
- Assorted fillings (cucumber, avocado, cooked shrimp, etc.)

Instructions:

1. Rinse brown rice under cold water until the water runs clear. Combine with water in a pot and bring to a boil. Reduce heat to low, cover, and simmer for about 45 minutes until rice is tender.
2. In a small bowl, mix rice vinegar, sugar, and salt. Heat until dissolved.
3. Once rice is cooked, transfer it to a large bowl and fold in the vinegar mixture. Allow it to cool.
4. Place a nori sheet on a bamboo mat. Spread a layer of rice, leaving space at the edges. Add fillings and roll tightly.
5. Slice and serve with soy sauce.

Spanish Fideuà (Spanish)

Ingredients:

- 2 cups fideuà noodles (or thin spaghetti)
- 4 cups seafood broth
- 1 lb mixed seafood (shrimp, squid, mussels)
- 1 onion, chopped
- 2 cloves garlic, minced
- 1 tomato, diced
- 1 teaspoon smoked paprika
- Olive oil
- Fresh parsley, for garnish

Instructions:

1. In a large paella pan or skillet, heat olive oil over medium heat. Add onion and garlic, sautéing until soft.
2. Stir in diced tomato and paprika. Cook for a few minutes.
3. Add fideuà noodles and toast for 2-3 minutes.
4. Pour in seafood broth and bring to a boil. Reduce heat and simmer for about 10-15 minutes.
5. Add mixed seafood and cook until seafood is tender and noodles are cooked. Garnish with fresh parsley before serving.

Tabbouleh (Middle Eastern)

Ingredients:

- 1 cup bulgur wheat
- 2 cups water
- 1 cup fresh parsley, chopped
- 1/4 cup fresh mint, chopped
- 1/2 onion, finely chopped
- 1 tomato, diced
- Juice of 2 lemons
- 1/4 cup olive oil
- Salt and pepper, to taste

Instructions:

1. In a pot, bring water to a boil. Add bulgur wheat and remove from heat. Let it soak for about 15-20 minutes until tender.
2. In a large bowl, combine parsley, mint, onion, and tomato.
3. Fluff bulgur with a fork and add to the bowl. Drizzle with lemon juice and olive oil. Season with salt and pepper.
4. Mix well and serve chilled or at room temperature.

Cheddar Rice (Southern U.S.)

Ingredients:

- 2 cups long-grain rice
- 4 cups chicken broth
- 1 cup sharp cheddar cheese, grated
- 1/2 cup milk
- 1/4 cup butter
- 1 onion, chopped
- Salt and pepper, to taste

Instructions:

1. In a pot, melt butter over medium heat. Add onion and sauté until soft.
2. Stir in rice and cook for 2-3 minutes until lightly toasted.
3. Add chicken broth and bring to a boil. Reduce heat to low, cover, and simmer for about 20 minutes.
4. Once rice is cooked, remove from heat and stir in milk and cheddar cheese until melted. Season with salt and pepper before serving.

Prawn Risotto (Italian)

Ingredients:

- 1 cup Arborio rice
- 4 cups seafood or chicken broth
- 1 lb prawns, peeled and deveined
- 1 onion, chopped
- 2 cloves garlic, minced
- 1/2 cup white wine
- 1/2 cup Parmesan cheese, grated
- 2 tablespoons olive oil
- Fresh parsley, for garnish
- Salt and pepper, to taste

Instructions:

1. In a saucepan, heat broth and keep it warm.
2. In a large skillet, heat olive oil over medium heat. Add onion and garlic, sauté until translucent.
3. Stir in Arborio rice and toast for 1-2 minutes.
4. Pour in white wine and stir until absorbed. Gradually add warm broth, one ladle at a time, stirring frequently.
5. When rice is nearly al dente, add prawns and cook until they turn pink. Remove from heat and stir in Parmesan cheese. Season with salt and pepper, and garnish with parsley before serving.

Garlic Rice (Filipino)

Ingredients:

- 2 cups cooked rice (preferably day-old)
- 4 cloves garlic, minced
- 2 tablespoons vegetable oil
- 1 tablespoon soy sauce
- Salt, to taste
- Green onions, chopped for garnish

Instructions:

1. In a pan, heat vegetable oil over medium heat. Add minced garlic and sauté until fragrant and golden brown.
2. Add cooked rice to the pan and stir to combine. Pour in soy sauce and season with salt.
3. Cook for 5-7 minutes, stirring occasionally until heated through. Garnish with chopped green onions before serving.

Egg Fried Rice (Chinese)

Ingredients:

- 3 cups cooked rice (preferably day-old)
- 2 eggs, beaten
- 1 cup mixed vegetables (peas, carrots, corn)
- 3 tablespoons soy sauce
- 2 tablespoons vegetable oil
- 2 green onions, chopped
- Salt and pepper, to taste

Instructions:

1. In a pan, heat 1 tablespoon of oil over medium heat. Scramble the beaten eggs until fully cooked, then remove from the pan and set aside.
2. Add the remaining oil and mixed vegetables to the pan, cooking until tender.
3. Stir in the cooked rice, soy sauce, and scrambled eggs. Cook for an additional 5 minutes, stirring occasionally.
4. Add green onions and season with salt and pepper before serving.

Sticky Rice with Pork (Laotian)

Ingredients:

- 2 cups sticky rice
- 1 lb pork, minced
- 3 tablespoons soy sauce
- 2 tablespoons fish sauce
- 1 tablespoon sugar
- 2 cloves garlic, minced
- 1 onion, chopped
- 1/4 cup green onions, chopped

Instructions:

1. Soak sticky rice in water for at least 4 hours, then drain.
2. In a pan, heat a bit of oil over medium heat. Sauté onion and garlic until fragrant.
3. Add minced pork, soy sauce, fish sauce, and sugar. Cook until pork is browned and cooked through.
4. In a steamer, steam the soaked sticky rice for about 20-30 minutes until tender.
5. Serve sticky rice with the pork mixture on top, garnished with chopped green onions.

Vegetable Fried Rice (Asian Fusion)

Ingredients:

- 3 cups cooked rice (preferably day-old)
- 1 cup mixed vegetables (carrots, peas, bell peppers)
- 3 tablespoons soy sauce
- 2 tablespoons sesame oil
- 2 eggs, beaten
- 2 green onions, chopped
- Salt and pepper, to taste

Instructions:

1. In a large pan or wok, heat sesame oil over medium-high heat. Add mixed vegetables and stir-fry until tender.
2. Push vegetables to the side of the pan and pour in beaten eggs, scrambling them until cooked.
3. Add cooked rice and soy sauce, mixing everything together. Stir-fry for about 5 minutes.
4. Add green onions and season with salt and pepper before serving.

www.ingramcontent.com/pod-product-compliance
Lightning Source LLC
LaVergne TN
LVHW081329060526
838201LV00055B/2529